Getting To Know...

Nature's Children

MOOSE

Judy Ross

SCHOLASTIC INC.

New York   Toronto   London   Auckland   Sydney
Mexico City   New Delhi   Hong Kong   Buenos Aires

Facts in Brief

Classification of the Moose

Class: *Mammalia* (mammals)
Order: *Artiodactyla* (cloven-hoofed mammals)
Family: *Cervidae* (deer family)
Genus: *Alces*
Species: *Alces alces*

World distribution. Found in northern regions of Europe, Asia, and North America.

Habitat. Northern forested lands near lakes or streams; may summer on the northern tundra.

Distinctive physical characteristics. Large palmate antlers on male; long legs; back slopes downward from high shoulders; bell-shaped fold of skin hangs under throat.

Habits. Solitary in summer; gathers in small bands in winter; swims in lakes to eat underwater plants; female raises calves (usually two) alone.

Diet. Leaves, twigs, bark, grasses, herbs, water plants.

Published by Scholastic Inc.
90 Old Sherman Turnpike, Danbury, Connecticut 06816.

SCHOLASTIC and associated logos are trademarks of Scholastic Inc.

ISBN 0-7172-6685-0

Printed in the U.S.A.

Edited by: Elizabeth Grace Zuraw
Photo Rights: Ivy Images

Photo Editor: Nancy Norton
Cover Design: Niemand Design

Have you ever wondered . . .

What comes to your mind when you think of a moose? Some people think of a coat-rack because the moose's upturned *antlers*—the huge bony growths on its head—look like a good place to hang a coat. Other people think of stilts because the moose's body is perched on top of long skinny legs.

A coat-rack on stilts! But if that's the way *you* think of a moose, you're in for a big surprise.

Moose may look awkward and clumsy, but don't be fooled by appearances. These animals are so agile they can disappear gracefully into dense forests without even making a sound.

Let's find out more about this striking member of the deer family.

Few animals in North America are as impressive as the long-legged moose. And the male has antlers that sometimes have been known to measure as much as 6 feet (1.8 meters) across.

Awkward Beginning

For the first few days of its life, a baby moose, or *calf,* has trouble getting around on its skinny, stilt-like legs. They wobble and buckle under the little moose, causing it to stagger unsteadily. But the calf gets stronger and steadier on its feet every day. By the time it's a week old, the calf might be able to beat you in a foot race. It also can swim, even at that early age.

A calf must become strong and steady on its feet very quickly so that it can run if danger threatens. After all, it doesn't yet have strong legs to kick with, or antlers it can use to scare off its enemies.

At birth, a baby moose's long legs are shaky, but soon the calf is able to run faster than you can.

Moose Turf

Most moose live in the forested areas on the edge of the Arctic in North America and Eurasia. But the *habitat* of some moose is found farther south, often near lakes or streams. A habitat is the place where an animal lives. Some moose even live in the treeless northern tundra, where the winters are often very cold.

*The shaded area
on this map
shows where
moose live in
North America.*

All in the Family

Moose are the largest members of the deer family. They're at least a head taller than their cousins—the elk, deer, and caribou. The male, or *bull,* is larger than the female, or *cow.* He can weigh as much as 1,200 pounds (535 kilograms) and stand more than 6 feet (2 meters) tall.

How can you tell the difference between a bull and a cow moose when you can't compare their size? It's easy. Only male moose have antlers.

Even though a female moose is smaller than the male, she is still as large as a horse!

Heavy Headed

Opposite page:
Waiting seven years for a full pair of antlers may seem like a long time, but it's just as well. What a staggering load a baby moose would have to carry if it suddenly sprouted a pair of antlers the size of a piano bench!

Imagine walking, running, and even swimming with a piano bench tied to your head. Sound impossible? Not for a bull moose. A fully grown bull moose's antlers can easily be about the size and weight of a piano bench! But while you might have trouble carrying around something so large and heavy, the moose doesn't even seem to notice its cumbersome headgear. It can lope easily through dense forest without smashing its antlers on trees or getting them stuck in branches.

Male moose don't start life with a handsome pair of antlers. During their first year, they grow only tiny brown buttons, the beginnings of antlers. The next year, the antlers are a bit bigger and they stick out like handles on either side of the moose's head. Finally, after seven years of bigger and bigger antlers, the male's headgear is fully grown.

Shreds of torn velvet still cling to the antlers of this moose. Some moose antlers can weigh as much as 80 pounds (36 kilograms).

Something's Missing

Male moose don't have antlers all year round. In early winter their antlers drop off. Often one antler is shed before the other, so the moose has to get used to being lopsided for a few days.

In early spring a new set of antlers sprouts. First tiny black knobs appear. These knobs are covered with a soft fuzzy skin called *velvet*. This velvet contains blood vessels to nourish the antlers and help them to grow.

By mid-July, the antlers are full size, and in early fall the velvet begins to fall off. During this stage the moose looks quite messy, with strips of ragged velvet hanging from its head-gear. To help loosen this fuzzy skin, the moose often rubs its antlers against trees.

Comparison of moose and elk antlers

Moose

Elk

The Big Stretch

Opposite page:
*A moose's long
legs come in
handy. When
threatened, the
animal can kick
out with either its
front or hind
hoofs—and it
doesn't often miss
its target!*

A moose is so tall that a three-year-old child would reach only to the animal's knobby knees. The moose's long thin legs account for most of its height. Having long legs is a big advantage for a forest dweller. They allow a moose to step easily over logs on the ground, reach up into trees for food, and wade through deep snow that would stop other animals.

If you're ever lucky enough to see a moose in the wild, stop and watch how it moves. It strides majestically through the trees and over fallen logs without slowing its pace. A moose on the move is a very graceful creature indeed.

The moose's long legs are also useful when it needs to defend itself or escape from an enemy. It can kick out to fend off a hungry wolf or, if that fails, it can outrun an attacker.

Like other members of the deer family, the moose has split *hoofs* for feet. A hoof is a hard covering of horn. As the moose walks over swampy ground, the split hoofs spread out slightly, providing more support for the moose's big, bulky body.

Sight, Sounds, and Scents

A moose's sleepy-looking, big brown eyes may be one of the animal's most handsome features, but a moose has very poor eyesight. Luckily its other senses are much sharper.

Its big ears are like those of a mule. Whenever a moose hears something that may mean danger, its ears stand up on end to catch the sound waves. Thanks to these effective sound catchers, a moose can hear much better than we can.

A moose uses its big nose to sniff the air. Its keen sense of smell can pick up the windblown scent of other animals long before the moose can actually see them.

With ears and a nose this big, hearing and smelling are two of the moose's strongest senses.

Moose tracks

19

Water Lover

Moose like to be near water where they can find food and escape from danger. They're strong swimmers and have even been known to dive underwater in search of a tasty plant. When a moose dives underwater, its *nostrils,* or nose openings, close to keep the water out of its nose, just as a submarine's hatches close before it submerges, to prevent water from pouring into the sub.

A river or lake is also a handy escape from black-flies and mosquitoes. In summer, a moose will stand neck deep in water to keep these pesky insects from biting it.

Water makes up an important part of the moose's habitat. Moose are often seen in or near it.

Big Eaters

It sometimes seems that a moose's day is just one long meal. In summer, juicy green leaves, twigs, and plants make up most of its diet, but its favorite food is water lilies. Much of a moose's water-lily munching takes place in the early morning or late in the afternoon. The moose stands partially submerged in the water and dips its nose under to tear the lilies from their stems.

This moose didn't have to wade in very deep to indulge in its favorite treat—water lilies.

During winter, when water plants are not available, the moose eats twigs. A full-grown moose may chow down 40 to 50 pounds (18 to 23 kilograms) of twigs a day. At the end of the winter, when a moose has already eaten most of the twigs it can reach, it may tear strips of bark off trees and eat that.

It's easy to tell if a moose has been feeding nearby. The trees will be twigless up to a height of several yards (meters). That's as high as a hungry moose can reach.

The word moose *is an Algonquin Indian word that means "twig eater."*

Cud Chewers

Like all of its deer family relatives, a moose is a *cud chewer.* This means that a moose chomps down food while it wanders around, but waits until it can rest quietly before chewing the food properly. A moose can do this because part of its stomach acts as a "storage tank" for unchewed food. When the animal rests, it brings the food, called *cud,* from this storage place into its mouth. Then it can chew in peace. On a hot summer day, a moose often lies down in a shady spot to chew its cud. In winter, it may just flop down in the snow.

A moose's menu includes leaves and tender twigs. With its long legs, this tall animal can easily reach high branches.

Winter Woolies

Many animals build nests, make *dens,* or dig *burrows* for homes. A den is an animal home made in a cave, near a fallen tree, or in some other cozy place. A burrow is a hole dug in the ground by an animal for use as a home. But when it comes to a home for a moose, this animal does none of these things. A moose wanders from place to place in search of food and sleeps wherever it happens to be. That may sound fine in summer, but what happens when winter comes?

Although the moose doesn't have a den to snuggle up in, it has no problem staying warm. It grows a thick two-layered fur coat in the late fall. An outside layer of *guard hairs* sheds ice and snow and keeps out cold winds. Beneath that, a layer of thick *underfur* keeps the moose's body heat from escaping into the cold air.

Even a moose baby has no problem staying cozy all winter. It's warmed by its thick fur coat—and its mother, always close by.

Moose Groups

Moose live alone most of the year, but sometimes in winter they gather in small groups to search for food. They scratch at the snow with their front hoofs to dig out bits of plants or roots. It doesn't take long before the snow gets tramped down by a group of moose. These flattened areas are called *yards.* But even in yards, the moose keep their distance—though they may feed near each other. And one rule always applies: The strongest and largest moose always get first choice of the best food.

Mating Season

For moose, fall is *mating season,* the time of year during which animals come together to produce young. Moose *courtship,* or behavior before mating, is a noisy and sometimes dangerous affair. To let a male know she's interested, a female bellows loudly. If two bulls hear her call, they may fight to win her. These fights often involve much clanging and smashing of antlers. But usually the weaker bull backs off before anyone gets hurts.

Opposite page:
In the summer, water plants are a steady item on the moose menu.

Overleaf:
It's a head-on collision when two bull-moose rivals meet.

A Moose Nursery

In the spring, the cow moose goes off by herself to find a place to give birth to her calves. She is very fussy about a nursery. It must be well hidden from *predators,* animals that hunt other animals for food. To insure safety, the mother moose looks for a spot among bushes and trees, usually at the water's edge where the trees are dense. An island makes a good, safe nursery. In this hidden spot, the cow gives birth to her calves. Usually she has twins, but sometimes she may have as many as three babies, or possibly only one.

A newborn moose calf weighs 22 to 35 pounds (10 to 16 kilograms)—about the weight of a large dog. The first sounds that the baby utters are low grunts, but soon it's calling loudly to its mother with a sound much like a human baby's cry.

A moose calf is born without spots, one of the few members of the deer family to do so.

From Wobble to Walk

For a few days, the moose calf lies on the soft ground in the secret hiding place, sleeping and *nursing,* or drinking milk from its mother's body. At first, the mother cuddles and nuzzles her calf with her soft, rubbery nose. But soon she begins to nudge it to get up and walk.

During the first year of life, moose calves and their mother are seldom apart.

First Outing

When it's about three days old, the moose calf is ready to venture out for a walk with its mother. It wobbles unsteadily behind her as she browses for food near thick bushes. If danger approaches, she will nudge her baby into the bushes, safely out of sight.

Before long the calf will begin nibbling on tender shoots and young buds on bushes and trees. And by fall, it'll no longer need to drink its mother's milk.

A moose calf's fur is reddish-brown. Adult moose are brownish-black, with lighter fur on their legs and belly.

Young Swimmer

If you ever see two moose swimming, look closely. One is probably a baby moose. A moose calf can swim when it's only a few days old, but it's not yet a strong swimmer. From time to time it may rest its chin on its mother's back until it has enough strength to paddle on its own again.

Moose are completely at home in the water. One day these twins will be powerful swimmers.

Watchful Mother

Wolves and bears see little moose calves as tasty dinners—so a mother moose must be especially careful to protect her babies. She relies on her keen senses of smell and hearing to alert her to any approaching danger.

If her calf is threatened, the cow moose lowers her head and snorts loudly like a horse. Then she may rear up on her hind legs and paw the air. If this display doesn't frighten off the enemy, she'll kick out with her long, strong legs and sharp front hoofs. Those legs are powerful weapons. A moose can cripple a wolf with one well-placed kick. And even if the calf's own father comes near, he'll get the same treatment as other intruders. A mother moose trusts no one near her babies.

A young calf will stay with its mother for at least one year before venturing off on its own.

Survival Lessons

Moose in the wild may live to be 20 years old, but there are many dangers and hardships they have to face along the way.

During its time with its mother, a calf learns all of the lessons it'll need to survive. It watches how its mother pulls up tender water lilies, and then it does the same thing. It also watches its mother so that it can learn which trees have good twigs and bark to eat. And whenever danger threatens, it learns how to fight off enemies. It even learns how to escape pesky flies and mosquitoes by hiding in the water. All of these lessons are important for a young calf. Only by learning them well will it be able to survive.

A moose's long legs and short neck make it difficult for the animal to reach its mouth all the way down to the ground. In order to get a drink, a moose usually just wades into the water.

Leaving Home

The moose calf grows quickly, and by its second spring it's ready to go off on its own. When it leaves, its mother begins to search for a hiding place to give birth to her next set of babies.

A female calf can be a mother herself at age three. A male calf won't mate until he's five or six years of age. That's when his antlers will be big enough for him to challenge other males in a mating contest. Until then, a young moose lives alone, wandering through the forest as it chomps twigs in the winter. And in the summer, too, it wanders, stopping now and then for a cooling dip in a lake and a water-lily snack.

Words To Know

Antlers   Hard, bony growths on the head of male moose.

Bull   Male moose.

Burrow   A hole dug in the ground by an animal for use as a home.

Calf   A baby moose.

Cow   Female moose.

Cud   Hastily swallowed food brought back up for chewing by cud chewers such as deer, cows, and moose.

Den   An animal home.

Guard hairs   Long coarse hairs that make up the outer layer of a moose's coat.

Habitat   The area or type of area in which an animal or plant naturally lives.

Hoof, hoofs   The hard covering of horn on the feet of moose, cattle, deer, and some other animals. Sometimes the plural of hoofs is spelled hooves.

Mating season   The time of year during which animals come together to produce young.

Nostrils   The openings in the nose that let air in.

Nurse   To drink milk from a mother's body.

Predator   Animals that hunt other animals for food.

Tundra   Flat land in the Arctic where no trees grow.

Underfur   Short, dense hair that traps body-warmed air next to an animal's skin.

Velvet   Soft skin that nourishes and covers a moose's antlers while they grow.

Yard   An area where moose gather in winter to find food.

Index

PHOTO CREDITS
Cover: J. D. Markou, *Valan Photos.* **Interiors:** William Lowry, 4, 17. /*Valan Photos:* Murry O'Neil, 7; Brian Milne, 13; Joseph R. Pearce, 21; Dennis W. Schmidt, 29, 38; J. D. Markou, 30; Thomas Kitchin, 32-33; Stephen J. Krasemann, 36-37, 42; Wayne Lankinen, 45. /*Ivy Images:* Norman R. Lightfoot, 9; Don Johnston, 22-23. /Bill Ivy, 10, 18, 26, 40-41. /*Visuals Unlimited:* Ron Spomer, 14; Rod Kieft, 25. /*Canada In Stock / Ivy Images:* Mario Madau, 34.

Getting To Know...

Nature's Children

OWLS

Elin Kelsey

SCHOLASTIC INC.

New York Toronto London Auckland Sydney
Mexico City New Delhi Hong Kong Buenos Aires

Facts in Brief

Classification of North American owls

Class: *Aves* (birds)

Order: *Stringiformes* (owls)

Family: *Strigidae* (typical owls)

           Tytonidae (barn owls)

Species: 18 species found in North America

World distribution. Depends on species. Owls are found worldwide, except in polar regions.

Distinctive physical characteristics. Very large eyes that point forward; ring of curved feathers surrounding each eye.

Habitat, Habits, Diet. Vary with species.

Most common North American species. Barred Owl, Long-eared Owl, Boreal Owl, Pygmy Owl, Burrowing Owl, Saw-whet Owl, Elf Owl, Screech Owl, Great Gray Owl, Short-eared Owl, Great Horned Owl, Snowy Owl, Hawk Owl, North American Barn Owl.

Published by Scholastic Inc.
90 Old Sherman Turnpike, Danbury, Connecticut 06816.

SCHOLASTIC and associated logos are trademarks of Scholastic Inc.

ISBN 0-7172-6685-0   Printed in the U.S.A.

Edited by: Elizabeth Grace Zuraw   *Photo Editor:* Nancy Norton
Photo Rights: Ivy Images   *Cover Design*: Niemand Design

Have you ever wondered . . .

Wise old owls probably appear in more cartoons, storybooks, songs, and advertisements than any other bird in the world. But they seldom have starring roles. Mostly, they perch on the sidelines looking serious and dignified and handing out good advice.

How did owls get their reputation for being so wise? Well, for one, their large eyes always seem to be studying things. And the feathery rings around their eyes remind us of the big, round eyeglasses that professors are often pictured wearing. In other words, owls *look* wise.

But the truth about real owls is that they're no wiser than any of our other feathered friends. Still, owls are amazing creatures. If you'd like to know more about these legendary birds, come fly into the pages of this book.

With its piercing eyes and no-nonsense look, this Great Horned Owl seems every bit the "wise old owl." Maybe it's just "wise" to the truth that owls, in fact, have only average bird intelligence!

Who's Who?

Owls are found everywhere on Earth, except in polar regions. From desert to forest to Arctic tundra, there is at least one type of owl for every *habitat,* or type of area where an animal lives.

But no matter where they live, owls are easy birds to identify. From the tiny Elf and Saw-whet Owls to the giant Great Gray and Snowy, owls look so much alike that even beginning bird watchers can tell when they've spotted one.

Like all birds, owls have feathers, hollow bones, and young that hatch from eggs. Yet owls are different from other birds in so many ways that they belong to their own special *order,* or group, of birds.

Most of us think of owls as rather large birds and, indeed, many are. Some, however, are no bigger than sparrows. The wee fellow shown here is a Saw-whet Owl. Tiny as it is, Elf and Pygmy Owls are even smaller.

Fluffy Feathers

From the top of their legs to the edge of their beaks, owls are covered with fluffy feathers. Some owls even have a thick layer of feathers all the way down to the tips of their toes. Owl feathers can be so soft and fluffy that if you were to close your eyes and feel them, you could easily mistake them for fur.

Most owls have dark gray and brown markings on their feathers. These colors provide good *camouflage,* they blend in well with their surroundings. An owl that is sitting still is very hard to spot. For that reason, owls—who hunt mainly at night—can rest, well hidden and undisturbed, all day long.

The fluffy-feathered Boreal Owl is named for the northern forests in which it lives. (The word boreal *means "of the north.")*

"Ears" That "Talk"

Opposite page:
Screech Owls, such as the one shown here, make a strange trembling sound up and down the musical scale. It's an eerie tune that's likely to pop the eyes of timid folks.

The little tufts that stick up on the top of some owls' heads look like ears or horns, and, in fact, they're usually called one or the other. Actually, the tufts are just special feathers and they serve a definite purpose.

When an owl is resting quietly, these feathers are only slightly raised above its head. The moment something upsets the owl, up shoot the feathery tufts.

If they stand up stiffly and a little forward, the owl is sending the same message a cat sends when it hunches its back and bushes out its tail: "I'm ready to fight for what is mine."

Standing up but leaning slightly outward, the tufts send a less aggressive signal: "You have no business here, but I'm prepared to put up with you so long as you behave."

And sometimes when an owl feels threatened and wants to avoid a fight, it'll completely flatten the tufts, as if to say, "Don't mind me, I'm just a little owl trying to get along."

Owl Eyes

Have you ever tried to catch the end of a baseball game just as the last rays of evening light were fading into darkness? Remember how difficult it was to see the ball?

That time of early night—dusk—is when most owls start their hunting. How can they find tiny gray mice when it's too dark for us to see a white baseball?

The answer is: an owl's eyes. They're enormous. If the eyes in your head took up as much room as an owl's, each of your eyes would be the size of a grapefruit! With such large eyes an owl can see much better in poor light than you can.

This Great Horned Owl and owlets, like all owls, have huge eyes that are especially equipped to catch the tiniest amounts of light. Owls, however, are color-blind, and see everything in shades of gray.

13

Most birds close their eyes by raising their lower lid.

Owls, however, lower their upper lid to close their eyes—just as you do.

But an owl can't shift its large eyes from side to side the way you can. Its eyes are fixed in their sockets just like the headlights of a car. When an owl wants to look around it has to turn its whole head.

This isn't a problem for an owl because it has a very long flexible neck underneath all those fluffy feathers. By twisting its neck, an owl can sit quite comfortably with its body pointed in one direction and its face in the other!

Many people think that owls can't see well in daylight. Actually, they see as well in daylight as you do. But they're *farsighted,* they don't see nearby objects clearly. In fact, day or night, an owl can't focus sharply on its own feet.

Like all owls, this Snowy Owl can turn its head around much further and much more comfortably than you can turn yours. But it can't turn it full circle!

14

Hidden Ears

Owls could never wear earrings. Their ears don't stick out the way yours do! Instead, an owl's ears are simply slits, sometimes very long, or small round holes on the sides of its head.

Even so, owls hear much better than you do. In fact, most owls hear so well that they can hunt just by listening for the tiny sounds a mouse or other rodent makes as it scuttles about on the ground.

Some owls have lopsided ears—one larger and higher than the other. The sound of a mouse's movements reaches each of these ears at a slightly different time. From this tiny difference an owl can tell exactly where the sound is coming from.

The special rings of curved feathers that surround each of the owl's eyes are called *facial discs.* These eye rings are very important to the owl because they help it hear. That's right: *hear!* The feathers in the facial discs are attached to muscles that control the shape of the ears. Just as a dog moves its ears to hear better, an owl moves these rings of feathers to locate sounds.

*Opposite page:
A Long-eared Owl
clearly displays
the rings of
curved feathers
found around all
owls' eyes.*

Swift and Silent

No matter how well an owl can see and hear, if it were as noisy as a jumbo jet when it flew, it would have a hard time catching anything!

To help muffle the sounds of flying, most owls' wings are well padded with soft, velvety feathers. And the feathers along the leading edge of the wing are fringed just like the teeth on a comb. These feathers help reduce the flapping noises that most birds make when they fly.

Try this simple experiment. Press the fingers of each hand tightly together and clap them against each other. Repeat the same thing but with the fingers of both hands spread out. Much quieter, isn't it?

Like your outstretched fingers, the fringed edge of an owl's wing allows most of the air to pass right through. With their special wings, most owls can fly almost silently.

Most owls are fairly fast flyers. This Snowy Owl, with its wingspan of about 5 feet (1.5 meters), can work up to tremendous speeds, but it needs a long take-off and landing run.

Talented Toes

Apart from wiggling them, most of us do very little with our toes. Owls, however, have many uses for their toes—perching, walking, grabbing, carrying.

All four of an owl's strong toes have hooked claws called *talons*. Just as you stretch your fingers out to catch a ball, owls spread out their talons to make a successful strike.

Owls do this better than most birds because of their movable outer toe. In fact, if an owl wants to, it can turn the outer toe around to the back so that it makes a pair with the back toe.

Back toe

Outer toe

Owl's foot

This young Barred Owl is in no danger of tumbling from its perch even if it falls asleep! Using two toes in front and two in back, the owl gets a solid grip on its resting place.

21

Mice on the Menu

Would you enjoy eating in a restaurant that served insects and mouse meat? You would if you were an owl! To an owl, such a menu would be positively scrumptious.

Owls are *carnivores*—meat is the only food that they eat. Owls never eat plants or seeds. The type of meat that an owl eats depends on how big the owl is and where it is hunting. A large owl that hunts in a meadow may eat lots of mice and rabbits, and even an occasional skunk. A small owl that hunts in a forest or desert may eat mice but it will probably eat plenty of grasshoppers, moths, and other insects as well.

Only insects, worms, and the smallest rodents have to worry about becoming a Pygmy Owl's dinner. The tiny Pygmy can weigh as little as 2 ounces (50 grams) and be no more than about 5 inches (13 centimeters) long.

Lone Hunters

Many birds feed in large groups called *flocks*. But owls need to hunt alone if they're to find enough food.

Take a minute to think about how you and your friends could collect the most eggs in an Easter egg hunt. The eggs are usually hidden in many different places. You would certainly find more of them if you and your friends spread out rather than stayed grouped closely together.

Small rodents—the objects of an owl's food hunt—live all over the meadow and forest floor. By spreading out and hunting alone, owls have a better chance of finding dinner.

Rodents Beware! The piercing eyes of a Hawk Owl are on the watch for a likely lunch.

An owl sits very still while it is hunting. Perched high atop a tree, fence post, or pile of rocks, the owl waits—carefully watching and listening for rodents. Sometimes an owl hunts by flying at a low height and watching the land below.

As soon as an owl spots its meal, it swoops silently and pounces. The force of the pounce causes the owl's legs to bend and its talons to close around its *prey*. Prey is an animal hunted by another animal for food.

A very hungry owl may have dinner right on the spot, but most carry their meal back to the safety of their perch. Mother owls carry their catch back to their babies in the nest.

As if hanging in mid-air, a Short-eared Owl seems to have spotted something interesting below. Perhaps an unsuspecting little field mouse?

A Neat Eater

Instead of picking the meat from the bones as you would when eating fried chicken, owls swallow everything, including fur and bones! Owls tear large prey into pieces before eating it, but if the prey is small enough, they swallow it whole.

With owls, the job of sorting out what can and what can't be digested goes on inside their stomach. Afterwards, the leftover bits of a meal are coughed up in sausage-shaped pellets.

It may sound messy, but an owl pellet is actually very dry and neat. The tiny bits of bone and fur inside the pellet are like pieces of a jigsaw puzzle. If we were to join enough of the pieces back together, we could figure out what the owl had eaten.

A Great Gray Owl pounces on prey that couldn't escape this bird's keen eye and razor-sharp talons.

Hard Times

When it comes to hunting, the owl has many advantages. But being an owl isn't always easy.

Like an unlucky person out fishing, an owl may spend hours without catching anything. On rainy evenings in particular, many owls go hungry. The damp ground muffles the sounds that rodents make, so it's harder for owls to locate them. Hunting is so difficult in the rain that most owls just sit it out and wait for better weather.

Most of the animals that owls hunt are *herbivores,* animals that feed on plants. If a year is too cold or too dry, there will be fewer plants and, therefore, fewer rodents. At such times some owls move to a new area to find food.

There are two separate families of owls: typical owls and barn owls. The heart-shaped face and light coloring that is common to barn owls gives this one a quite distinctive look. The barn owl's name comes from the fact that these birds often nest in the dark corners of barns.

Who...Who...Who's There?

Every owl has its own section of forest or meadow that it calls home. Known as the owl's *territory,* it is the area the owl lives in and defends from intruders.

Owls use a variety of calls to warn off unwelcome visitors. Some hoot, some whistle, and many have a call that resembles a shrill laugh. If you listen carefully on a clear night you might hear owls calling to each other. The owls in an area recognize one another by sound, and they know where their neighbors' territories are. As long as they are careful to hunt only in their own backyards, the owls remain good neighbors.

This Burrowing Owl has made its nest on a golf course. It's not known whether the person who made the sign did so out of concern for the owl or the golfers!

Finding a Mate

In late January, a male owl's nightly calls get louder and more frequent. This is the owl's *mating season,* the time of year when owls come together to produce young. The male's calls announce his ownership of a territory and his interest in attracting females. Sometimes a female answers with her own song, and the two sing an owly duet.

Except for being a little larger, most female owls look just like the males. Even a male owl sometimes has trouble telling the difference, and he is so protective of his territory that he sometimes may mistakenly try to chase away the very female he has attracted. It often can take a lot of hooting before the male realizes that the new bird is a female and not an unwelcome male!

To impress their new mates, male owls often perform trick flights or dance-like movements on a branch. And just as a man may give chocolates to his sweetheart, some male owls woo their mates with gifts of tasty mice!

Unlike some owls, a male Snowy has no trouble knowing when he has attracted a female. She is easily recognizable by the dark markings on her feathers. Male Snowies are almost pure white.

Nesting Time

When it comes to nest building, owls aren't very talented. In fact, very few build nests at all. Instead, owls often lay their eggs in a hole in a tree, in a crack in a cliff, or in a slight hollow they scratch into the ground. Many owls move into an abandoned nest that some other bird built the year before. There is even a Burrowing Owl that makes its home in the underground burrows of prairie dogs.

Some owls lay their eggs when the ground is still covered with snow. This may seem like a chilly time to start a family, but it means that the babies will *hatch,* or break out of their eggs, in spring—the time of year when there are plenty of rodents to feed them.

A Great Horned Owl mother guards the nest while the father is away hunting for food. Some owl parents choose a new mate every year, but many stay together for life.

*Baby Short-eared owlets await the hatching
of yet another brother or sister. Each egg
hatches at a different time.*

Happy Hatch-Day!

A female owl may lay as few as three eggs or as many as twelve. The number depends on the type of owl she is and on the amount of food she has had available to her. A female owl that is eating well will lay more eggs than one that is not.

The mother owl lays one egg and then waits a few days before laying the next. As a result, each egg hatches at a different time. Every baby owl, or *owlet,* has its very own hatch-day!

The eggs need both time and warmth to hatch. For several weeks, the father owl hunts for two, while mother spends all her time sitting on the eggs to keep them warm. To do this more effectively, the mother owl often plucks out some of the feathers on her underbody to make bare patches. That way, her body heat goes directly from her skin to the eggs. Her feathers don't get in the way.

Hungry Babies

Owlets are born with a covering of soft white fluffy feathers called *down*. Snuggled up to its mother and wearing its fluffy down coat to keep in the heat, an owlet stays cozy even in the chilliest storms.

Owlets grow very quickly and have huge appetites. A week-old owlet can eat much more for its size than an adult would.

For that reason, the father owl is kept awfully busy finding food for his family. Fortunately, owls are expert hunters of mice and other small animals. In fact, owls are much better mousers than any cat. Even so, the father owl may end up having to hunt both night and day to keep up with the enormous appetites of his young family.

A Snowy owlet, like all owl babies, is always ready for the arrival of its next meal.

Next step: flying. But until they do, these Saw-whet owlets spend quite a bit of practice time moving around the branches near their nest.

Devoted Parents

When an owlet is three or four weeks of age, its fluffy down starts being replaced by longer, gray and brownish feathers. The owl babies now need so much food that their mother may leave them for short periods to help their father hunt. As the owlets grow, the increasing number of dark feathers helps keep the youngsters well camouflaged while their mother is away.

Owls are very protective parents. If a hungry weasel or a curious person approaches the owlets, the parents swoop down, threatening the intruder with their sharp talons. Even the tiny owlets help to scare off enemies by hissing, snapping their beaks, and puffing up their feathery coats.

Long before they're able to fly, owlets move onto nearby branches and plants. Often people find these owlets and take them home, thinking they're lost. But the owl parents know where their babies are and are taking good care of them. It's important to leave them alone.

Growing Up

Owls learn to fly the same way that you learned to walk or ride a bicycle—with lots of practice and lots of bumps!

As the owlets develop their flying skills, the parents encourage them by dangling a tasty meal at a distance. Through practice, the young owls gradually learn to hunt for themselves. By fall it's time for them to leave their parents and find territories of their own.

The first year of an owl's life is the most dangerous. With so much still to learn about the world, many of the young owls don't survive their first winter. But those that make it to celebrate their first hatch-day have a very good chance of living to celebrate many more.

By puffing out its feathers to look threatening, a young owl can scare away an intruder.

Owls and Us

Owls are awesome birds and helpful, too. They do an important job for farmers by catching insects and rodents that like to eat crops. Farmers would have a serious problem with mice, rats, and other pests if there were no owls.

Because most owls are active at night, it's harder to watch them go about their daily routine than it is to watch other birds. But people are learning more and more about owls. Bird-watching groups conduct "owl prowls," walks meant to find and study owls in the wild. And many people are interested in protecting owls, especially the *species,* or kinds, of owls that are *endangered,* threatened with dying out.

But there still are many things we don't know about the ways and habits of owls. So the next time you're out in the woods, stop, take a careful look around, and give a few hoots. You may discover yet another fascinating fact about owls.

Words To Know

Camouflage   Coloring and markings on an animal that blend in with its surroundings.

Carnivore   Animal that eats flesh.

Down   Very soft, fluffy feathers.

Endangered   Threatened with being destroyed or dying out.

Facial disc   The ring of curved feathers that surrounds each of an owl's eyes.

Farsighted   Able to see distant objects better than near ones.

Flock   A group of animals that lives and feeds together.

Habitat   The area or type of area in which an animal or plant lives naturally.

Hatch   To break out of an egg.

Herbivore   Animal that eats mainly plants.

Mating season   The time of year when animals come together to produce young.

Order   A grouping used in classifying animals and plants.

Owlet   Baby owl.

Prey   An animal hunted by another animal for food. A bird that hunts animals for food is often called a bird of prey.

Rodents   Animals such as mice, rabbits, and gophers that have teeth especially good for gnawing. Rodents are common prey of owls.

Species   Class or kind of animal that has certain traits in common.

Talon   Claw of an owl, eagle, or other bird of prey.

Territory   Area that an animal or group of animals lives in and often defends from other animals of the same kind.

Tundra   Flat land in the Arctic where no trees grow.

Index

PHOTO CREDITS

Cover: Stephen J. Krasemann, *Valan Photos.* **Interiors:** Bill Ivy, 4, 11, 35. */Valan Photos:* Michel Julien, 7, 19, 24, 28; Wayne Lankinen, 8, 16; Stephen J. Krasemann, 15, 37; Albert Kuhnigk, 20, 38, 44; Dennis W. Schmidt, 23; Brian Milne, 27; J.A. Wilkinson, 41. */Network Stock Photo File:* Ken Carmichael, 12, 32./ *Federation of Ontario Naturalists,* 31. */Hot Shots:* Doug Latimer, 42.